Dinosaur Dig

Ian Rohr

Published by
Sundance Publishing
33 Boston Post Road West
Suite 440
Marlborough, MA 01752
800-343-8204
www.sundancepub.com

Copyright © text Ian Rohr
Copyright © illustrations Cliff Watt

First published 2005 by
Blake Education, P.O. Box 250, Glebe NSW 2037, Australia
Exclusive United States Distribution: Sundance/Newbridge, LLC

Dinosaur Dig
ISBN 978-0-7608-9831-4

Photo Credits
p. 14 photolibrary.com; pp. 16–17 APL/Corbis/Louie Psihoyos; p. 18 Science Photo Library; p. 19 photolibrary.com; p. 20 Transparency no. 17838-f (photo by H. W. Menke, 1898), supplied courtesy of the Library, American Museum of Natural History; p. 26 photolibrary.com; p. 27 AAP; p. 28 © Mitchell Gerber/Corbis; p. 29 © Louie Psihoyos/Corbis

Printed by Nordica International Ltd.
Manufactured in Guangzhou, China
February, 2019
Nordica Job#: CA21900147
Sundance/Newbridge PO#: 229250

TABLE of CONTENTS

The Buried Age of Dinosaurs

What if you found a giant rock that was millions of years old?

Not exciting enough? What if that rock held the skeleton of a meat-eating dinosaur? Or a dinosaur that no one had ever seen before? Sound better? Let's go dig up some dinosaurs!

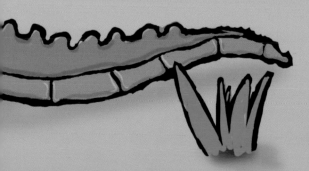

Dead and Buried

Dinosaurs ruled Earth for more
than 160 million years. But abou
65 million years ago, they died o
All that is left of them are **fossil**

For a long time, people though†
fossils were the remains of giants or
dragons. Then, in 1824, one scientist
figured out that the fossils were actually
from **extinct** reptiles. Many dinosaur
fossils have been identified since
then. But there are many more
discoveries still to be made!

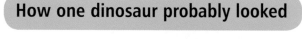

How one dinosaur probably looked

What Is a Dinosaur?

scientists agree that dinosaurs were
-based, four-legged reptiles. The word
saur comes from the Greek language.
eans "terrifying lizard." But unlike
rds, whose legs are out to the sides of
r body, dinosaurs' legs were directly
w their body. Dinosaurs came in
dreds of forms. Some ate meat; others
grass and leaves. Some were gigantic;
others were the size of a chicken!

Model of a dinosaur

A Passion for the Past

So what is it about dinosaurs that interests us? Is it that some of them were fierce killers? Is it that some were so huge? A tyrannosaurus rex tooth is larger than your hand and can still cut through flesh after 70 million years in the ground!

Q: What do you call a dinosaur that drops all the dishes?

A: *A tyrannosaurus wrecks.*

Teeth of a tyrannosaurus rex

Dinosaur Time Line (mya = millions of years ago)

Dinosaurs and mammals appear.

Birds appear.

Triassic Period	Jurassic Period

251 mya   203 mya   146 my

A meteor crater in Arizona

Maybe it's the mystery of how they became extinct. Did a string of massive volcanic eruptions kill them all? Or did a huge meteor hit Earth, destroying everything around?

Dinosaurs become extinct.

People appear.

etaceous Period

65 mya

Now

Fossil Finder Top Spots

Dinosaur fossils have been found in many places, from burning deserts to frozen Antarctica. But as this map shows, some places are top spots for digging up dinosaurs.

Lyme Regis, Southwest England
Fossils of pterodactyls and plesiosaurs have been found at this site.

Plesiosaur

Velociraptor

New site

The Karroo Basin, Africa
The fossils of different kinds of sauropod dinosaurs have been found here. Some are 200 million years old.

Sauropod

**Flaming Cliffs,
Gobi Desert, Mongolia**
Fossils of some of the best-known dinosaurs, such as velociraptors, have been found here.

**Como Bluff, Wyoming,
United States of America**
Remains of such dinosaurs as the 89-foot-long diplodocus were found here.

**Yunnan Province,
China**
Six dinosaur skeletons were found at this site in 2004.

Diplodocus

Valley of the Moon, Argentina
Fossils of dinosaurs as well as ancient crocodiles and mammals have been discovered here.

Winton, Australia
Over 3,000 footprints made by over 300 different kinds of dinosaurs have been found here. The footprints were made 95 million years ago.

Dinosaur Wars

It's easy to get it wrong when you're putting together a dinosaur.

Edward Cope and Othniel Marsh were fossil hunters and friends. Cope was proud of his latest dinosaur skeleton. He'd put it together himself. But Marsh just laughed at him. Cope had put the dinosaur's head on the tip of its tail!

From that day on, the two dinosaur hunters hated each other.

Dinosaur Kingdom to Dinosaur Graveyard

Como Bluff, Wyoming, can be a tough place. Summers are hot, and winters are freezing. But during the Jurassic period, when dinosaurs lived there, the weather was always warm. Many dinosaurs were **preserved** in Como Bluff.

How Animals Become Fossils

1

2

3

4

Figure 1 – The animal, in this case an iguanodon, dies.

Figure 2 – The flesh rots away, leaving only the bones. The bones lie undisturbed, or they are moved by animals or water.

Figure 3 – Sediment, or fine soil, slowly covers the animal's remains. Over a long period of time, the sediment hardens and becomes rock. Meanwhile, minerals in the sediment enter the bones.

Figure 4 – The iguanodon's bones are now made up of minerals. These make the bones stronger and help to preserve them. Sometimes the earth gets worn away, and the fossilized bones become exposed. But some bones may lie deep in the ground until they are dug up someday.

Fossilized bones

A Great Discovery

In 1872, a railway was being built through Como Bluff. Two workers cut through some bones that were unusually enormous!

The workers wrote to Othniel Marsh and told him about their find. Marsh sent a team right away to start digging.

Paleontologists looking for bones at Como Bluff

The Battle over Bones

For about a year, Marsh had Como Bluff to himself. During that time, his team dug up 60,000 pounds of dinosaur bones. But Cope soon heard of the rich find and sent a team to dig, too.

Othniel Marsh

Edward Cope

The **rival** teams spied on each other and kept their guns close by. When a team finished at a site, they smashed all the bones to stop the other team

from studying them. Marsh and Cope fought a bitter war over a hill of bones.

The Death Pose

At first, scientists thought that dinosaurs could hold their necks backwards like the apatosaurus pictured below. But the dinosaurs' necks only bent backwards when the muscles loosened after death.

Jurassic Jackpot

Como Bluff is a fossil hunter's treasure chest. Many dinosaurs and hundreds of early mammals have been found in this part of Wyoming. In fact, the remains of more than 300 **species** have been discovered.

Not all of the fossils at Como Bluff have been dug out yet. New bones keep poking out!

Some of the fossils found at Como Bluff

Dinosaurs at Como Bluff

Allosaurus
- high IQ
- meat eater
- 16 feet tall

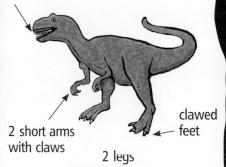

large teeth

2 short arms
with claws

clawed feet

2 legs

Apatosaurus
- low IQ
- plant eater
- 69 feet long

long neck

long tail

4 legs

Ceratosaurus
- high IQ
- meat eater
- 20 feet tall

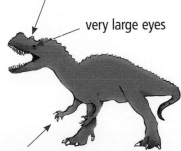

horn on nose

very large eyes

2 short arms

2 legs

Diplodocus
- low IQ
- plant eater
- 148 feet long

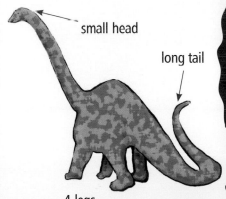

small head

long tail

4 legs

What Lies Beneath Your Feet?

It's hard to move when you've been in the same spot for 70 million years!

Finding a dinosaur skeleton is just the start. It's a long trip from the dig to the lab. Helicopters, bulldozers, and dynamite are all used to get a dinosaur back on its feet again.

Finding Fossils

You have to know where to look to be a good fossil finder. Creek banks, dry riverbeds, and cliff faces are all good places to search. That's because they contain sedimentary rock, where plant and animal fossils can be found.

Sedimentary rock along a coast

Sedimentary Rock?

Sedimentary rock is the best rock for fossil hunting. It has layers made up of tiny bits of stone, sand, and mud that have turned into rock. Many creatures can be preserved within these layers.

Q: What do you call a fossil that doesn't want to work?
A: *Lazy bones!*

Calling All Fossil Hunters!

Do you have what it takes to find a dinosaur fossil? Well, think about this. Only about 30 T. rex skeletons have ever been found—and just one was discovered by an actual scientist! Fossils have even been found by kids. Eleven-year-old Chantell Bury found a skeleton while on vacation. And 13-year-old Wes Linster found the fossil of a whole new kind of dinosaur. So start digging!

A dinosaur fossil found by a farmer in 2004

Digging Out Dinosaurs

Some fossils can be dug out in minutes. But others take months. Most fossils are covered by a thick layer of rock. At some sites, explosives blow up the rock, and bulldozers cart it away.

Often the whole block of rock, with its bones, is cut out from the earth. Then it's taken back to the lab, where the bones are carefully removed.

Removing fossils from rock

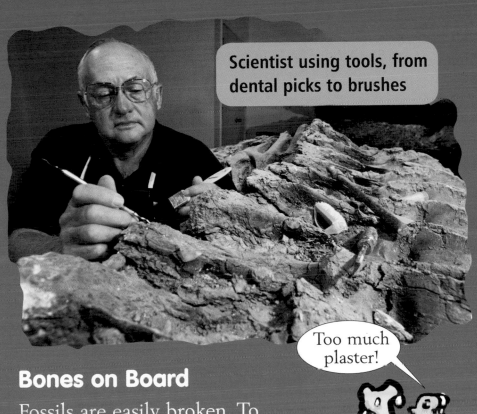
Scientist using tools, from dental picks to brushes

Too much plaster!

Bones on Board

Fossils are easily broken. To protect them while they are being moved, small bones can be sprayed with glue. Big bones are often wrapped in plaster. Back at the lab, special tools are used to free the fossils from the glue, plaster, or rock.

A protected fossil

Giant Jigsaw Puzzles

Edward Cope wasn't the only person to put a dinosaur part in the wrong place. Putting a dinosaur back together takes skill, patience, and a lot of time.

Using photos and drawings, the bones are laid out on the floor. Then the skeleton is put back together from the ground up.

Dinosaurs Roam Again

Movies like *Jurassic Park* have re-created the dinosaur world. Using computers and imagination, filmmakers can bring dinosaurs back to life.

Steel supports holding the weight of a skeleton

Most bones are too **fragile** to become a skeleton in a museum. So scientists make a **mold** for each of the bones. From these molds, they create plaster copies of the bones. Because it is rare to find a complete dinosaur skeleton, scientists usually make the missing parts.

Can you Dig it? 29

Fact File

My grandfather was a dinosaur!

In a way, dinosaurs aren't extinct. Birds are believed to be descendants of the dinosaurs. Some dinosaurs even had feathers.

Triceratops and torosaurus, the largest of the horned and frilled dinosaurs, were as long as 33 feet and weighed up to 7 tons. The biggest torosaurus skulls are 9 feet in length.

Now, if I could just lift my head.

One of the largest meat-eating dinosaurs discovered is the gigantosaurus from Argentina. These massive munchers were nearly 46 feet long.

My teeth are sharper than a steak knife.

Glossary

extinct no longer existing

fossils the remains of plants or animals from an earlier time protected in soil or rock

fragile easily broken

mold a hollow form in which something is shaped

preserved kept safe from damage or destruction

rival competing

species a category of living things of the same kind and the same name

Index